Beyond the foreshore...

John Lockyer...
Putting Dover Over

Encouraged by

Published by
John Lockyer

ISBN 978 – 0 – 9930116 – 0 – 3

Printed by A.R. Adams & Sons (Printers) Ltd
The Printing House, Dour Street, Dover, Kent, CT16 1EW
Email: info@adamsprinters.co.uk

To Dame Vera Lynn,
with heartfelt appreciation,
John Lockyer.
November 12th, 2014

FOREWORD

I have never met anyone with such a love of Dover as the author of this memoir, Beyond the Foreshore. After reading its interesting pages I am sure you will agree.

John Lockyer was not born in Dover but, at a young age, moved to Snargate Street where his parents ran a restaurant next to the Royal Hippodrome. His early years, in the 1930s were exciting days of exploring the town and its environs. Days of unravelling in the military secrets of fortified establishments including the Western Heights and Dover Castle and times of fun and games at the docks where he was not supposed to venture.

These were the days when youngsters were safe wherever they went, an era when young people did not stay at home watching television or playing digital games.

Today, a wheelchair-bound octogenarian living in Sussex exile, John remembers in graphic detail his active childhood in the town but also has dreams of recapturing the importance of Dover that it enjoyed in yesteryear. Reading his words leaves no doubt about John's strong views about patriotism, education and Christianity. But more than anything else he writes with enthusiasm that one day Dover will become a city.

Terry Sutton MBE
Honorary Freeman of Dover

"The Tivoli Theatre", circa 1890, before being re-named "The Royal Hippodrome." 32 Snargate Street is the three storey building on the left foreground. Photo, Dover Museum.

Beyond the foreshore

PART 1

From my first moments on Dover's beach, as an inquisitive five year old in 1933, I knew that all that I ever wanted was all around me waiting to be explored and understood. My parents had chosen to open a small restaurant – 28 "covers", at 32 Snargate Street, which happened to be next to the Royal Hippodrome Theatre on its West side, with the outfitters Gigg and Tournay on its East side. Both of these buildings made the restaurant look like its name, "The Nook."

"The Hippodrome" itself gave my imagination new wings, as did the cliff face opposite, which, as it is now, was festooned with greenery and divided by the great brick-lined moat leading to the Drop Redoubt and the Citadel. On the West side of the moat was the "South East Postern", from which every evening an army bugler would emerge. He then crossed the moat by fixed wooden stairways to a stone platform opposite the postern. There he called soldiers back to Shaft Barracks, then overlooking much of Snargate Street.

As my bedroom afforded the view of the cliffs, with a live theatre next door, Dover itself became very much a magical theatre of dreams. It remains so to this day. Most Dovorians would understand this living in a wonderful place that deserves to be known much better than somewhere to pass through. My purpose is to "put Dover over" as something more than "The Gateway to England." The government refusal to the privatisation of the port of Dover is a golden opportunity to "put Dover over". Let's begin.

Few historic places can match Dover. Evidence of regular trading in the Bronze Age is captivating. Look at the 74 acre Iron Age fort upon which the Romans built their lighthouse – and later, after 1066, the Normans built their "Key to the Gateway to England". In 2016 and 2017, those who care will celebrate the anniversaries of the "Siege of Dover Castle" and the "Battle of Sandwich", when Hubert de Burgh prevented foreign domination of Britain. He loved Dover. Get to know about him, I have. Hubert de Burgh is on the internet.

As a small boy in Snargate Street I developed a keen taste for history. Old Dovorians I met were eager to tell me all they knew. My mother made sure that any written material on Dover was given to me. Besides this, at the age of seven when I became a pupil of St Mary's School for Boys, Queen Street, I was allowed great freedom to roam far and wide in and around Dover. Few children can do this today! Fortunately, other parents of adventurous young boys in Dover thought likewise to mine.

The Preussen aground in Fan Bay before its destruction by heavy seas, December 1910. Most of its cargo of one hundred pianos was saved but the remaining cargo of cement was abandoned. Photo, Dover Museum.

One of my first quests was stimulated by a shop in Snargate Street. Amos, a notable photographer, had his studio not far from my home. The *"Preussen"* – a five masted steel built, square rigged ship – the largest of its kind in the world, ran aground beyond the Eastern Arm in 1910 after a collision with a channel steamer. Heavy seas battered it into five thousand tons of scrap metal. At great risk, Amos recorded every sequence in photographs. By studying the photographs, we knew where to find out if any trace of the wreck remained.

It may seem surprising that boys as young as seven could predict tidal cycles accurately if they visited Dover's foreshores as often as we did. We had chosen to visit Fan Bay at the lowest spring tide in combination with fair weather. This meant waiting some time, as the right combination also had to occur at a time outside regular school activities. We had one problem. How to get the best view of the wreck? It could be difficult and dangerous. We were not reckless.

At Fan Bay, the cliffs were about two hundred feet high and sheer. When we eventually had the best conditions, only two of us were able to walk to the cliff top beyond the Eastern Arm and the Camber, Fearnley Parsons accompanied me. His father, like mine, was a caterer whose business was based opposite the former stage coach terminal in Snargate Street. "The Milestone Café" had the original milestone, "72 miles to London". Fearnley was proud of this.

Together we carefully worked out possible safe places to get to the cliff edge. Overhanging top soil spelt danger. To minimise this, we lay head first and some distance apart, while wriggling forward until we could peer down the cliff face. The thrill of being above herring gulls circling in the updraft was rewarding and unforgettable, as was the scent of herbs in the cliff top grass where we lay. Had we come to the right place? All we could see was kelp seaweed and half submerged boulders of chalk, directly below us. We widened our search.

To our right, something attracted our attention. It was white. We repositioned ourselves for a better view. It was a section of steel plating that while twisted and streaked with rust, was painted white.

We could see about fifteen feet of it. All we saw suggested that we were looking at the starboard bow inside of the crew's quarters, as this was common practice on merchant shipping. Officers would be at the other end of a ship. Yes, we had found a trace of the *Preussen*, a quarter of a century after the wrecking. It is still there!

Before radar, collisions in the Strait of Dover were unfortunately frequent in foggy conditions. Ships used their sirens operated by steam or compressed air. Dover had a powerful fog horn that sounded like a pre-historic monster in agony. Dover Harbour Board tugs, the *"Lady Brassey"* and *"Lady Duncannon"*, would tow collision victims into the harbour at high water and carefully beach them on the foreshore. At low tide, emergency repair work would be carried out before ships were re-floated and taken to a dry dock elsewhere. With other boys, I watched these procedures with great interest. Steel plating behaved like tissue paper in collisions!

Another great interest to most Dover boys was The Dover Patrol, 1914-1918. Snargate Street people told me about calm days when smoke from dozens of warships blanketed the harbour and much of the town. The ships interested me. There were destroyers to escort cross channel traffic, minelayers and armed trawlers – all capable of anti-submarine work. The largest ships were the "monitors", designed for use in shallow waters. They carried long range heavy guns, up to 15 inch calibre, in rotating turrets. The American Civil War introduced this type of "ironclad". It was named *"USS Monitor"* – the name became generic. Monitors are now obsolete.

Newly commissioned *HMS Glatton*, one of eight monitors in Dover Harbour on the evening of September 16th, 1918, was in operational readiness for the bombardment of the Belgian Coast.

It was moored, close to other warships, when an explosion in the midship 6 inch gun magazine started a fast-spreading oil fuelled fire, which threatened a truly catastrophic blast, capable of causing sympathetic detonations in ships nearby. Dover itself was in peril!

H.M.S Glatton in dry dock before going to Dover. Note the anti-torpedo bulges that made it difficult to sink, as ordered by Vice Admiral Sir Roger Keyes on September 16ᵗʰ 1918. Photo, Imperial War Museum.

Many lives were lost on *Glatton*. Vice Admiral Sir Roger Keyes, quickly grasped the situation. Attempts to open the seacocks to scuttle *Glatton*, though heroic, were futile. The Admiral ordered torpedo attacks to "sink the fire". *Glatton* reluctantly capsized and sank after a two hour struggle, becoming an obstacle to shipping until 1925. Stripped of its superstructure, *Glatton's* five thousand ton hulk was raised with great difficulty and moved to a deep water trench. That trench is now built over as Dover's Eastern Docks. Think of *HMS Glatton* next time you pass through.

In 1936, the huge car ferry port did not exist. Dover boys full of curiosity were aware that the wreck site would be accessible at low spring tides when little more than two feet of water covered it, enabled the recovery of bits and pieces of *Glatton* and its warlike contents. Such recoveries were strictly forbidden however, boys would tell parents "I'm going fishing". Perhaps we were naughty and foolish – but always well prepared to avoid obvious hazards.

Canvas shoes with thick rubber soles and bathing trunks were used for push net fishing to catch shrimps and prawns. Thus clad, three of us set out with four foot long bamboo rods to the wreck site. It was not far from "Dover Industries" Wharf. The sea was calm the air warm. Fearnley Parsons was first in the making of a find – porcelain insulators. Mine was only a 303 rifle cartridge – but Bobby Adams, another Snargate Street boy, found a Mills Bomb.

Fearnley had a large tin box full of insulators. He was pleased with his lucky dip as we walked home. Just past the swimming baths, we froze with terror at a sudden metallic clatter! It wasn't the Mills Bomb, but the tin of insulators. "Let's take the bomb to the Police Station" was our unanimous decision. When we entered the Police Station, then below the Maison Dieu Hall, we assumed an air of innocence. "We found this on the beach sir". Whether the Police Sergeant believed this, I will never know. Perhaps he had been like us?

Beachcombing was a pastime for most Dovorians, young and old. The laws of flotsam and jetsam applied. By handing in the bomb – crown property and "flotsam", we complied with law on that occasion. Beachcombing was always a pleasure for me – a part of the magic of Dover – of which there is more to tell.

The Dover Harbour Board Tug, "Lady Brassey" on the Wellington Dock Slipway. This ocean going tug built before the Great War, was in service until the 1950's. It was much admired. Photo, the author.

Beyond the foreshore

PART 2

Snargate Street in the 1930's, still had the character of a "last chance" emporium which it was at the time of the "Grand Tour", from the 1760s to beyond the 1890s. I have already mentioned its function as a Stage Coach Terminus. Even when railways arrived in Dover and steamships were becoming dominant, Snargate Street retained its primacy as a street for all trades and retailers.

Snargate Street, circa 1820 close by "The Grand Shaft" access long before wharfage improvements in Wellington Dock and road widening, led to the demolition of buildings shown on the right of this picture. Photo, Dover Museum.

When the "White Cliffs Experience" was being created, I was asked to provide a detailed list of all the businesses I could remember clearly from the 1930s and their locations which I plotted out on a simple map. I still have the original draft of this information in case that which I gave in the 1980s has been lost. Even if that were so, my vivid memories would suffice.

My father's small restaurant, "The Nook", at 32 Snargate Street, in its immediate proximity to the "Royal Hippodrome" raised much interest in the "White Cliffs Experience" planning team. They, like many other Dovorians wanted details of this lovely 600 seat theatre, which is no more than a fond memory for anyone over 75. I'm 86. My first visit to the Hippodrome was Christmas, 1933, for a Pantomime. I cannot remember its title, however the young girl performers from a local dancing school impressed me. The late great Maurice Chevalier's song sums up how I felt – and still feel. "Thank heaven for little girls!"

More about "The Royal Hippodrome". Yes, you can find out much on the internet but this is personal. By 1934, my father was asked to provide suppers to performers each of whom had different food preferences. A happy outcome was the provision of a "box" for family use – free of charge. For me, it was "the icing on the Dover cake" for six years! The first visit to our box, together with my mother and four year old sister Primrose, was in August 1934. I can remember each precious moment.

Sitting in a "circle" seat, as I did in 1933 gave me an excellent view of the stage. Our box, one of four – if my memory is correct – was more than a viewpoint. It was an all-embracing experience for me. Although the stage is seen at an angle from a box the whole of the auditorium is in a surrounding view. As our box was on the West side, almost in line with the Orchestra Pit we could see into the "Wings" on the East side of the stage, while we were closer than before to the action on our side. The reactions of the audience could also be seen.

To me, this interplay in live theatre cannot be in any way supplanted by spectacular stage design or lighting, as seen on

A wartime audience in "The Royal Hippodrome", enjoying the show. Note the boxes. This is the only available photo that shows them. Our box in the 1930's, was the one on the left. Photo, Rex Puttee.

television or cinema. To watch a darkened orchestra pit pierced with a beam of bright light, as the musicians come through their door beneath the stage is for me, a moment of high expectation. I have never been disappointed.

Next time you go to a theatre, try a box. Stroke the velvet sill as you wait and be surprised as I was. The Royal Hippodrome was altogether surprising.

"Stage Door Johnnies" in Dover, had to walk round the block into Northampton Street. A stone's throw away was the Wellington Dock. In 1933, electric tramcars rattled by the stage door. This was a sound which I would hear at bedtime, whenever I slept in the "Ships Room" – the fourth bedroom of 32 Snargate Street. Sometimes I used a glass to listen to music in the theatre. Waking up was likely to bring another surprise – the arrival of a ship in the Wellington Dock.

I have already mentioned my keen interest in ships. The Strait of Dover offered the pleasure of "spotting" a ship that was famous, such as the *"Pamir"*, sister-ship of the ill-fated *"Preussen"*, or the Cunard Liner *"Mauretania"*, with its four funnels. The *"Bremen"* – a Hamburg Amerika Liner called regularly moored in the East of Dover Harbour. Passengers were taken to and from the *"Bremen"* and other liners, by the Harbour Board tender, *"Lady Saville"*. Wellington Dock was limited to ships up to three thousand tons displacement.

While named to honour the famous Duke as "Lord Warden of the Cinque Ports", Wellington Dock had its origins in Elizabethan times, after Henry VIII's great pier was built from the West side of the small medieval tidal harbour known as "Paradise".

Overlooking Snargate Street, a view from the Shaft Barracks, showing Wellington Dock as it was before land reclamation and the construction of Northampton Street. Snargate Street retained all its buildings on the dockside, while Northampton Street had buildings on both sides for most of its extent. Photo, Dover Museum.

The king hoped that his pier would enable large warships to operate at any state of the tide. He built Archcliffe Fort to defend this strategic asset. Sadly, his engineers failed to take the Westward shingle drift into account. This would be disastrous.

As storms pounded the pier, shingle was carried seaward along its West side until it reached the pier head. Liberated from its obstruction, the shingle spilled across Dover Bay to make today's seafront. Storm after storm piled it higher. Ships could not enter the "Paradise" Harbour which had become part of a land-locked semi-tidal lagoon. By the time of Queen Elizabeth I, Snargate Street, dominated by the lagoon, faced redundancy.

The challenge to Dover as an important seaport was met with a heroic response. Evidence of this, is Dover's Marinas formerly, the Wellington and Granville Docks. James I, who knew about Dover's unwanted beach, granted a Royal Charter to Dover Harbour Board in 1606. The history of Dover Harbour is inspiring. That's another reason for me to "put Dover over". As this account of a Dover boyhood, involves the Harbour Board in the 1930's I must tell how Snargate Street boys regarded the Wellington Dock as an adventure playground. Dover Harbour Board did not! They appointed a dock policeman.

"Billy Bubbles" – that's what we called him. Rumour had it that his real name was Burville. We, the Snargate Street boys justified his employment by Dover Harbour Board – especially when shipments of timber arrived in Wellington Dock from Scandinavia and Germany. Most of this timber was destined for "Crundalls Timber Yard", less than a mile away. Horse-drawn waggons carried the timber from the dockyard, where it was stacked in orderly eight foot piles that attracted us boys.

Timber piles were essential for "rites of passage" in full view of "Billy Bubbles" – provided that he was on the other side of the dock by Waterloo Crescent, just over a hundred yards away. The "rite" was limited to boys over twelve, strong enough to make timber plank bridges between at least six of the eight foot stacks. Younger boys would support the "rite" as soon as "Billy Bubbles" appeared and the candidates began their test of nerve, crossing all the bridges, shouting his name. There was another "rite" that I passed.

The domain of "Billy Bubbles" and our adventure playground. Left, Granville Dock, above centre, Wellington Dock, bottom right, the Tidal Basin. Photo, Dover Museum.

After the commencement of the building of Admiralty Pier in the late 1840's, which checked the shingle drift blocking access to the Tidal Basin and until the 1870's when sufficient ship berthing facilities were available on Admiralty Pier, these locations were used for embarkation and landing passengers and goods. Timing for these activities depended entirely on the tides. With the completion of Admiralty Pier, the two docks ceased to be embarkation and disembarkation points for passenger ships, but continued with goods traffic.

The "rite" involved small barges known as "lighters" that were used for dock maintenance and were moored on rope springs. Carefully releasing the springs making sure that you could haul the lighter back to the dockside you pushed it clear in full view of "Billy Bubbles". I qualified at the age of 10. Poor old "Billy" never caught anyone. Whether he reported our pranks to the Harbour Board, I do not know.

The "Granville Dock" – another consequence of Henry VIII's mistake, was at the Western end of the lagoon, which after a "cross wall" – a causeway, had been built became a separate entity. The remaining larger part of the lagoon became "The Pent" which, until Wellington's time lacked a locked gate and water retention improvements. It is noteworthy that the River Dour flowed into the Eastern end of The Pent. Snargate Street had a future again.

The causeway that divided the lagoon, developed in width after the Royal Charter. Old prints of Dover show this clearly, together with Granville Dock and its warehouses. Locust Beans – a cattle feed – was a favourite snack that we could scrounge from them. The "causeway" had lost its original buildings and was dominated by "Hawkesfields Coal Wharf". Three impressive "Stothert" and Pitt Level Luffing Cranes, stood ready to unload coal from Newcastle.

Granville Dock was used by Trinity House Pilot Boats, *"Pathfinder"* and *"Pioneer"*, which resembled steam yachts. They were beautiful – as was the Southern Railway Steamer *"Biarritz"* – a veteran of the 1914-1918 War another frequent visitor. This was because most out of service cross channel steamers, regularly spent time in Granville or Wellington Dock. While we had much pleasure from these fine ships, for us boys, the spritsail barge *"Haughty Belle"* was tops!

Spritsail barges were a common sight in Wellington Dock as working ships. *"Haughty Belle"* was a yacht – a beautiful floating home with fresh paintwork and gilding. Impeccable ropework and sails, together with decking that would dazzle an Admiral, was graced by a three foot high brass bird cage, in which a gorgeous macaw perched and chattered. I last saw *"Haughty Belle"* in Dover in 1939.

St Mary's School for Boys, Queen Street. A strict but happy place,
where Archibald John Wellden was headmaster for many years.
Thanks to him, I had an interesting career. Photo, Dover Museum.

into the school yard. Turning left, you came under cover. Above you, at first floor level, jutting out from the main building, was the staff common room – resting upon steel girders and supported at its outer corners by cast iron pillars. From the common room, teachers were able to spot troubles and respond quickly.

Boys were told not to loiter under the cover of the common room, except in heavy rain. A hand bell signalled the start of each school day. Outdoor clothes were hung on numbered pegs in cloakrooms at the lower end of the yard, before over two hundred boys assembled in their classrooms for the morning prayers and a hymn. When each school day ended prayers and hymns marked the event. Christianity celebrated without shame in the 1930's.

St Mary's School for Boys did not have an assembly hall as most modern schools have, to enhance the effectiveness of headteachers. Archibald John Wellden, Headmaster in the 1930's, overcame this deficiency by taking classes himself, as frequently as possible. There were eight classrooms, known as "standards" – according to the level of ability of pupils aged between seven and fourteen. Pupils in standard six could expect to sit for a Grammar School Scholarship. The remainder would leave school at fourteen.

"Archie" as we called him, ensured that "square pegs went into square holes". He encouraged the natural talents of pupils evaluating them on "course work" rather than frequent tests or examinations. His aim was to teach boys to think. Correct answers did not impress him as boys moved up to "Standard Four".

Upon giving a correct answer to an oral test, a boy risked a painful caning if he failed to provide a clear reason for it. This was how the boy would "be taught to think". "Human Rights" were not taught! Duties were! This would appal today's educationalists.

From a historical perspective "Archie's" methods are justifiable.

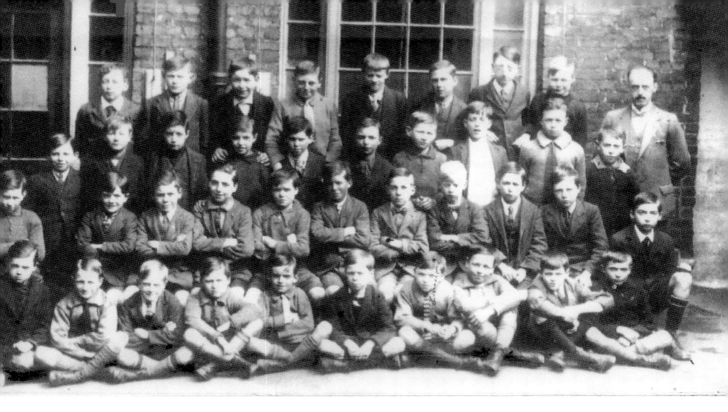

This photograph dates from shortly before my time at St. Mary's School for Boys, Queen Street. The school entrance from the yard is on the left. Boys in the group are aged between eight and fourteen and are under instruction by Mr Biggs for carpentry and joinery. The older boys had the opportunity to learn cabinet making to an advanced standard. Photo, Hollingsbee Collection.

Unless you completely absorb an educational process, so that it becomes "a train" of linked up thought that you retain and develop, academic degrees will mean nothing. Passing examinations by remembering answers is not the right way. "Swotting" is not thinking. In time, all answers and qualifications gained that way, will be gone. "Archie" did his boys a good turn.

Another important principal this headmaster taught, was love and loyalty whether in the family or at school in the place where you lived or the nation where you were born. Patriotism and nationhood were not politically incorrect ideas. We were taught to admire heroes like Hubert de Burgh or Captain Scott. "The Annals of Dover" was commended reading.

This window in the Lady Chapel of St. Mary the Virgin Cannon Street, sums up the values of its own schools. On the left, King Alfred the Great, patron of learning. On the right, Hubert de Burgh, whose life of faith, fortitude and good works was exemplary.

St Mary's boys had one special hero, who lived in a large house at the top of Queen Street. During Summer, he would emerge just before our school day began and walk with confidence down the middle of the street on his way to the seafront. As our hero had a slight limp we thought that he was a 1914-1918 war veteran. With a peaked cap and reefer jacket he was master of a speedboat.

To us he was Mr Walker. Not until September 1940, did we know him as Councillor John Walker. His famous speedboat, we all knew very well. They were inseparable. "The Shooting Star" was probably the fastest of any speedboat in the South East of England in the 1930's. Councillor Walker handled his beautiful speedboat with such skill and daring, that his six paying passengers realised that they were enjoying a superb "white knuckle-ride", When the annual Dover Regatta took place in August, Shooting Star was the popular high attraction in an event featuring a De Havilland biplane, which began proceedings with an aerobatic display and hair raising low flying.

Councillor Walker was ready in Shooting Star as the display ended. His powerful speedboat engine growled like a lion. Then everyone along the seafront heard a mighty roar as Shooting Star challenged the biplane circling overhead. This was a contest. The object was to demonstrate the superiority of air power over sea power. The biplane pilot had a good supply of three pound bags of flour to prove it. In "bombing speedboats" year after year, Shooting Star won!

Boating was a popular pastime. Councillor Walker had rowing boats for hire, as did the Brockman family next to him. Mr Betts, opposite Granville Gardens, made a living that way. Brockmans had two fine motor launches that cruised the harbour. Summer holidays for us boys meant going to help these boatman. I will tell how we did.

Looking up Queen Street towards the home of our "Shooting Star" hero, Councillor Walker, who always walked down the middle of the roadway. Photo, Dover Museum.

Beyond the foreshore

PART 4

Before detailing the happy relationship that boys like me had
with boatmen, I want to tell readers about the dominant feature of
the wonderful place where I spent so much of my childhood – Dover
Castle – 74 acres of it. It was in clear view from schoolroom windows
and looked like a walled city. In Holy Week, it evoked Jerusalem and
the hill of Calvary nearby. Stanley Spencer, the mid 20th century artist,
experienced similar feelings about Cookham on Thames.

*Dover Castle, as seen from the junction of St. James Street and
Woolcomber Street. The ancient Church of St. James, now a war torn
ruin, was once the meeting place of the Cinque Ports Barons. To the left
of its intact West Doorway is a narrow steep passageway – a short cut to
Castle Hill and the steps to Canon's Gate. Photo, the author.*

Having said that, all Dover boys found their imagination healthily stimulated by the Castle. This was clear to me, as my circle of friends grew. Among them, a new friend Dennis Willett. His father had a shoe and leather goods repair business, almost opposite "The Milestone Café", close to Dover's former stagecoach terminus and home of Fearnley Parsons. Dennis, a Roman Catholic altar boy, loved playing his piano accordion and adventuring. He also loved anything driven by steam, Southern Railway's "Lord Nelson" locomotive most of all.

The only admission charges to Dover's Castle, were to the Keep and Underground Works – with adult supervision compulsory. This allowed boys like us to explore beyond the limits set by the "Ministry of Works" – responsible for the ancient castle structures and the "War Department", who had barracks, tunnels and other installations necessary in the event of major conflict, much of this totally out of bounds and guarded by the Military Police. These conditions were a welcome challenge to our trio Dennis Willett, Fearnley Parsons and me. We took all the risks that could have had serious consequences without a single thought – as most normal boys do.

Having been warned by older boys who had sneaked into forbidden places on the famous "Western Heights" and within the Castle grounds, we were highly alert and ready for action at the first available chance. We found that chance in the Northeast corner of the Castle grounds. We couldn't believe our good luck – not a "redcap" in sight and an open door, revealing a stone spiral staircase descending into the gloom. Without further ado, we were in – glancing briefly behind us as the darkness began to engulf us. To our surprise the darkness melted away, twenty or so feet down, as electric lights were installed the rest of the way down to a passageway.

"This stairway must be in regular use" said Fearnley as we entered the passage.

Dover Castle from the North. Originally an Iron Age fort, this site was first developed by the Romans. Their lighthouse, the "Pharos" is top centre of this photograph, next to the restored Saxon Church, St Mary in the Castle. At the bottom of the photograph, in the centre, is where the French undermined the gateway during the siege of 1216 and broke into the Outer Bailey. Hubert de Burgh led the defenders to victory. Following the siege, Hubert de Burgh strengthened this Northern extremity and built the "Constable's Tower" – today's main gateway – mid right of the photograph, with "Canon's Gate" – top right. The brick lined moat can be seen on the upper left of this photo. It was where we should not have been in the 1930's. It was an adventure. Notice the trees. They make the difference and should be conserved.

29

This photograph, by special permission of English Heritage, shows part of the prohibited area known as "Hudson's Passage" which our mischievous trio entered in the 1930's. By courtesy, Derek Leach, O.B.E. Photo, John Wells.

It was not as well-lit as the spiral stairway and curved to our left until daylight came through an opening before us. Where are we? The answer came dramatically and unexpectedly. We were in a brick-lined moat, overgrown with hemlock and bramble. While this was not pleasing, the sounds from above were alarming – the clatter of hob-nailed Army boots and voices made us search for cover in the moat. Would we be caught by the redcaps? And our parents?

The dry moat floor was uneven. This was to our advantage – together with the cover of plant growth. Keeping out of sight, we held our breath as the men began to come out of the passageway into the dry moat, about sixty feet from where we were then hiding. They were lining up ready to take orders – to search for us? No! They were not Military Police but Seaforth Highlanders, under the command of a Senior NCO not searching for us, but under training in the use of their

Through frequent visits to Dover Museum in the Market Square, boys like those who shared my inquisitiveness, discovered that the boatmen of Dover were a necessity because of the shingle bank that blocked access to the old Paradise Harbour. King Charles II had to land on the shingle bank in 1660, as had most cross channel travellers since the reign of Elizabeth I. "Faring Boats" were the only means of embarking or disembarking passengers and goods all the year round. A risky business.

Dover Beach in the 1830's, close to the place where King Charles II landed in 1660. Note the horseman, probably a Customs Officer. Faring Boat traffic was nearing its end at this time.
Photo, Dover Museum.

What of the boats that were used? What of the faring boatmen? Having sought the answers, I now appreciate the pride of boatmen that I worked with. What I have deduced concerning the boats, is that they were similar to the Royal Navy ships tenders called "Pinnaces", capable of working in open sea conditions and "crewed" by a minimum of four oarsmen (with single oars). Many of these boats had a sail. A coxswain, to steer and supervise, made the fifth member of the crew. These faring boats were designed to hold a profitable payload, but sadly, Dover archives record that faring boatmen, desperate to make a living in hard times, were tempted to "rip-off" travellers who had no alternatives. Smuggling by faring boats was not uncommon.

This state of affairs continued well into the 19th Century. Spare a thought for faring boatmen as you board a ten thousand ton "roll-on – roll-off" car ferry – even if you opt for "Le Shuttle".

"Messing about in" – and with boats, in our case was getting them in and out of the water, also to help their sometimes anxious passengers, to get in and out of the boats. Shingle makes launching troublesome. Strips of greased hardwood with a loop of rope to grab at one end, worked wonders. We laid them to make a slippery pathway so that as the boat moved forward, the rearmost strip was speedily transferred to the front.

This "moving slipway" technique demanded alertness and teamwork. For safety, we never stood in the path of the boat. Taking a boat up a shingle incline also needed the strips, plus a winch. Carrying oars, rudders and cushions back to the storage lockers, was another chore for us. As a reward, we were taught basic seamanship. Visiting yacht owners soon recognised us as boat minders when they came ashore to go shopping. "Can I try her out sir?".... "Yes sonny, take care". This was good responsibility training.

It may surprise you or not, that my association with boatmen and boating – as related on the previous page – began in the Summer of 1935, when I was seven and a half. Perhaps I gave adults a misleading impression for two reasons. My lanky physique and deceptively sober

Captain Matthew Webb, the first man to swim the Channel in 1875, had his monument set up in front of Dover's most prominent building – apart from Dover Castle, "The Burlington Hotel" – later "Burlington Mansions" luxury apartments. Its massive bulk provided a "reference point" for German long range guns at Sangatte and it was hit many times. One hit had caused part of the tower section to collapse while a man was using the toilet. Rescuers found him clinging to the cistern which saved his life but not his dignity. Photo, Dover Museum.

Soldiers of the Dorset Regiment were in the Shaft Barracks in 1935. One of them had presented a hand carved regimental badge in "mother of pearl", to my father as a mark of appreciation of his restaurant and because he was a veteran of the Great War. The 4th/7th Royal Irish Dragoon Guards fought the first battle involving British soldiers. My father had then survived a dreadful casualty rate. He displayed an oil painting of the Royal Irish Dragoons in a charge, on his restaurant wall. Shortly after the outbreak of the Second World War, my father was asked to take charge of catering for Dover Garrison's Officer's Mess. They knew what to expect.

What about homelife? You may well ask, that since my mother made sure that my youthful energy was not wasted or my schoolwork neglected. She also planned another change in my life, as she knew that I loved music. One day I was getting ready for school, happily singing "I'm forever blowing bubbles". Mother opened the bedroom door suddenly. "You can sing in tune", she said and would take me to sing to Leonard Baggerly, Organist and Choirmaster of St Mary the Virgin Church! I went regularly to this church, also to its Sunday School.

While the prospect of becoming a choir boy did prompt some anxiety in the late Summer of 1935, I was too busy with other interests – not forgetting homely chores that my mother set for me to do. These varied throughout the seasons of the year. In the Winter, three fireplaces needed clearing and made ready for use. This was a creative exercise, as I wanted efficient combustion and always had a pleasurable buzz when this happened. It did every time. I also had an unhealthy interest in basic pyrotechnics, making things go bang!

As we lived in a three storey building, with four "flights" of stairs and two landings my mother chose to have removable stair carpets, held in place with brass stair rods. My job, year in and year out, was to keep everything clean and shiny. Shopping was another regular chore. Sometimes my father sent me on errands, to get items for use in the restaurant, while one of his regular customers, much enamoured with

Much had been published on the possibility of a Train Ferry Service between Dover and Dunkirk. The idea of a train ferry took shape in Victorian times, but was never carried out. Surprisingly, it was not planned to be within the harbour, East of the Admiralty Pier. Instead it was to be beyond that pier to the West, close to Archcliffe Fort. Dover Museum has an illustration of it.

As railways had vastly improved commerce and the mobility of people, this inspirational plan for a train ferry between Britain and the Continent of Europe took shape under Sir John Fowler in 1869. After much discussion by Parliament, the plan was abandoned as there were too many problems. Photo, Dover Museum.

The first knowledge we had concerning the new Train Ferry project, was the arrival of a large "bucket chain" dredger from Holland.

Its task was to cut a deep water channel that would allow the new ferries to leave or enter at the lowest spring tides. The dredger had its name displayed in large black letters, high up on its superstructure that operated the bucket chain. None of us boys could pronounce "RIJN". The noise it made was agonising. We were worried that it was frightening the prawns that we were trying to catch from "North Pier".

Aerial view of the Train Ferry Berth and the entrance to the Tidal Basin and Docks. The Lord Warden Hotel and Admiralty Pier (Marine Station Approach) top left. Note the shingle beach, top left. Henry VIII's great pier was located in the area of this 1937 photograph.

48

North Pier marked the easterly side of the channel, dug through the shingle bank blocking entry to Paradise Harbour. This channel was unreliable until 1850, when major stone and concrete work, plus the commencement of "Admiralty Pier" overcame the problem of shingle drift. A moulded concrete tablet in a new sea wall, celebrated this – "MDCCCL". As yet, in 1935, higher Roman numerals were "double Dutch" to us – just like the name of the dredger.

My friend, Fearnley Parsons solved "MDCCCL" as we walked home one evening from North Pier, via the Clock Tower. "My dad can catch cooked lobsters".

As we couldn't catch prawns on the North Pier, using hoop nets on a line, we decided to try push nets on the sandy bottomed strip of water available to the East of the North Pier, going three hundred yards up to the Prince of Wales Pier. We had excellent catches of prawns, the length of a man's finger. Were they refugees from the dredgings?

Catching prawns with a hoop net and line, can be effective and rewarding provided you are nearer to the water – as from a low jetty, with plenty of corks fixed on the line to keep it clear of the net itself, so that the prawns can gather around the smelly fish bait. Using a long pole with a fork of wood or metal at the end, you gently engage a cork nearest to the surface of the water. It's up to you then. The quicker you swing the pole upwards – the prawns (who are very quick) are in your net! We always cooked our prawns as soon as possible.

Boys like us, fished by choice. Men, such as Miss Chilson's father, had to. Mr Chilson lived in an ancient stone cottage, halfway up an alleyway on the West Side of Limekiln Street. I had already seen his sturdy clinker-built fishing boat. It looked like hard work to me. Meeting Mr Chilson the first time is an enduring memory. He was having a frugal breakfast of boiled shore crabs, pulling off their legs and scooping out their shells with a spoon.

The Royal Hippodrome had "Drama Seasons" that reflected the harsh realities of a world without a welfare state (except Nazi

Germany) – provided that there, you were only fortunate if you supported the National Socialist redemption programme. "Love on the Dole" was a play that my parents did not want me to see. Nellie Wallace, Harry Tate Junior, Sandy Powell and other popular "Music Hall" performers were "O.K." In spite of this, I saw "Love on the Dole" and all the others.

To see how the "other half" of 1930's Britain was living, you only had to spend a few short moments watching well-heeled people embarking from Admiralty Pier or arriving on the "Golden Arrow" at Dover's Marine Station. It was worth paying for a platform ticket to see happy travellers on their way to exotic destinations all over the continent and beyond.

For me, the cross channel steamers, though small in comparison with today's giant ferries, spelt romance and sublime beauty. The motor ship, *Prinz Albert*, Dover to Ostende, caught my imagination most of all, as I watched a large touring coach being loaded on "after deck" by a "Stothert and Pitt" crane. One image I shall never forget is the Southern Railway's steamer, *Canterbury*. I was on the extension of Admiralty Pier with a fierce gale blowing. Approaching the then open Western Entrance, the *Canterbury* heaved, plunged, side-slipped on massive waves, until within the harbour, it glided majestically and safely to its berth.

The master of a passenger ship has always had full responsibility for the safety of all on board. Mindful of the ferry disasters of modern times, the captain and crew of the *Canterbury* achieved the highest standards of seamanship in unexpected circumstances. I found this inspiring.

While describing the *Canterbury's* entry to Dover Harbour in brief dramatic terms, there is much more to be said for the benefit of those who have little knowledge of the hazards faced. Being at the narrowest and shallowest part of the Strait of Dover, means that the speed of ebb and flow tides is much greater at Dover than elsewhere in the English Channel. The massive harbour itself, deflects the tidal currents to

On its maiden voyage from Ostende to Dover, October 4ᵗʰ, 1937, the Belgian motor ship "Prins Albert" broke the speed record and profoundly influenced marine engineering thereafter. During World War II, it had a distinguished career, sailing far and wide in important operations including D day. The beautiful ship ended its service in 1968.

Built for the "Golden Arrow" luxury service between London and Paris, the Southern Railway steam turbine ship "Canterbury" set high standards when it began its thirty five years service in peace and war in 1929.

speeds of more than 8 mph – an important factor in the calculations of seafarers approaching harbour. No less important is wind speed and the nature of ground swell.

This remarkable painting by Charles Pears, Chairman of the Society of Marine Artists, is reproduced by the kind permission of its owner – an experienced seafarer and close friend. It was an emergency of wartime that meant taking risks. John Masefield, Poet Laureate, 1930-1967, on seeing the painting in 1945, wrote to the artist – "the best painting of a really dangerous and ugly water I have ever seen". I couldn't say more!

The artist titles this painting. "From the age-old menace which carries no escort but providence." A footnote adds – "A steamer running to the port for shelter, flying signal flags – men dangerously injured." From its orientation and configuration, the harbour is possibly Dover, at its Western entrance. Charles Pears did not confirm this.

Yes, there were storms, when the breakwater was like a wide waterfall, but memories are generally illuminated by sunshine. The death of King George the Fifth coincided with ominous events abroad. Fred Astaire sang, "There may be trouble ahead". Dover "faced the music" and danced at the Grand Hotel by Granville Gardens. By 1936, Dover had a new "state of the art" Fire Engine, "Rosetta" – the name given to my new little sister, born that year.

Archibald John Wellden – always dressed in a blue-grey suit, with a trefoil gold tiepin that had dark, light blue and white inset stones – not forgetting his commanding waxed moustaches, assessed the international situation adroitly. He planned an all-embracing curriculum that would produce a firm and enduring sense of the vital importance of the United States of America. I would revel in this imaginative study programme so much that my work books were preserved for many years.

With power struggles and warfare in so many parts of the World in the late 1930's, current affairs became a regular addition to Mr Wellden's curriculum. Friday afternoons were chosen for a review of World events. Questions were answered. Most boys found current affairs interesting. Unfortunately, some chose to "act out" notorious Gestapo Secret State Police activities during playtimes. You risked arrest and being suspect under interrogation in the Boiler House alleyway. It was a topical version of "you're it!" Some boys were frightened.

The imports of timber from Germany, raised some questions as to whether spies might be operating to check Dover's military potential. When the huge "Graf Zeppelin" overflew Dover in the late 1930's all of us boys stood in the schoolyard to watch it pass. Was it on a photo mission? When a German ship arrived in Wellington Dock, our eyes were on the crew. The Germans were probably briefed to appear benign, as on Sunday afternoons they would lounge on the after deck where a swastika flag was displayed. An accordion played and the Germans sang and smiled. Yes, I'm sure this was ordered.

Coinciding with one German ship's arrival, copies of "Mein Kampf" were on sale at Timothy Whites shop in Biggin Street – in good English of course. Again the Germans were playing a public relations card. When Neville Chamberlain brought "peace in our time" from Hitler, Dover's pubs soon ran out of beer. Perhaps some, who knew the truth, were drowning their sorrows instead. My parents had no illusions. Dover was preparing for war. Mysterious pylons appeared – "Radar". Death Rays?

Early one evening in November 1938, an urgent call from the mother of my cousin Vivian, asked my parents to meet him at Marine Station. Cousin Vivian, then a sixteen year old grammar schoolboy, was having to make an unexpected return from Germany while on an exchange visit. Could we look after him for two days? My parents agreed. Vivian was a "big brother" to me. I was pleased.

After my father brought Vivian home in a taxi, it was nearly midnight but I was allowed to come downstairs because Vivian had important first-hand news about revenge attacks against Jews after a German diplomat had been murdered in Paris. His description was blood curdling. We didn't go to bed in the hope of peace in our time after that. However, I lived life as eagerly as ever.

My sister Primrose became a welcome companion to me by the time she was five. The walks with her nanny, Miss Chilson, gave us a "common ground". Primrose was remarkably literate reading aloud. She also had a perceptive sense enabling the creation of stories about people we could see from the first floor bay window that commanded a wide view up and down Snargate Street. I shall relate some of our fanciful assumptions about the people of Snargate Street in the next instalment of this series.

Beyond the foreshore

PART 7

Snargate Street, East. Dover Express Office, third building on the left. Burlington Hotel in the distance. From a 1910 coloured postcard, Dover Museum.

Two photographs of the Royal Hippodrome before 1896, known as the "Tivoli" show 32 Snargate Street on its left. The first floor bay window of number 32 is the place which enabled my sister Primrose and I to have a splendid view of the street. To our left, looking down was the theatre foyer. Beyond we could see the opposite side of the street, as far as the Masonic Hall with its impressive round headed windows – a place of mystery to us.

To our right, looking down we could watch people looking into Gigg and Tournay's outfitters which specialised in naval badges, beautifully worked in gold wire. The furthest building visible on the other side, was brick built and large having on its side wall, facing us, white capital letters, declaring "BON MARCHE" (For a good bargain). The paint looked old and worn. Evidently our French neighbours came for day trips long before the Great War.

My sister Primrose sensed the romance of this fascinating street, with its gas lamps hanging from elegant iron arches at hundred yard intervals. The theatre next door "grabbed" her fertile imagination with its splendidly attired "Commissionaire" welcoming theatregoers, often in evening dress, as they alighted from their cars – not too many in those hard times. The "Page Boy" was my sister's favourite romantic character, in Snargate Street.

She called him "Boy Blue". This was because the colour of his uniform and that of the Commissionaire, was sky blue with gold trimmings. Very glamorous.

This smart lad, who made sure that performers were on stage in good time, could be seen most days dashing down the street. He was often to be seen walking and talking with his mother. She was appropriately called "Mrs Blue". I believe that this lady unfortunately suffered from a problem that I have had for the last twenty-six years – very painful osteo-arthritis. My sister called it an "acid", which was the way she walked.

If you are musical and can remember the well-known "Baccarole" from "Tales of Hoffman" – that was the rhythm of Mrs Blue's walk. Primose would "la la" this music letting Mrs Blue "conduct" her. Usually, I would join in, trying to work out a suitable simple harmony. Were we cruel doing this? Sadly, as children, we only saw the funny side of things.

*Inside the North Entrance to the Western Heights fortifications, via the
Military Road. Fortunately, this fascinating tunnel, which dates from
the 1850's, still exists – although now "boarded up" and disused. A new
cutting nearby allows access to motor traffic, while the old tunnel awaits
the day of restoration that we all hope for. Photo, Dover Museum.*

The gun emplacements were empty but we could see the iron semi-
circular traverse tracks upon which the gun carriages were mounted
pivoted at the muzzle end to allow a field of fire of 90 degrees. Brick
lined gun crew and magazine chambers were protected by earthworks.
After the war, the battery became a pleasant cliff top walkway. Bravo
to that. Dover has many similar assets.

Beyond the foreshore

PART 8

The huge Western Heights fortifications – death traps to deter invaders, remain, in their greater extent, out of bounds to the public. Ironically, some parts of the fortress are used to detain would be immigrants while English Heritage has enabled guided tours to take place in the Eastern Drop Redoubt area which boys like me called "the hidden city". Unrealised potential is Dover's story. The eight hundredth anniversary of the momentous events of 1216 and 1217 will soon be upon us. Interest is evident of this on the internet.

"A study of constancy". That's how Hubert de Burgh's life has been described. "Tubby" Williams, history and maths teacher at St Mary's School for Boys, told us about Hubert de Burgh's heroic defence of Dover Castle in 1216. He didn't need to tell us. We went on our own pilgrimages to the place where the French, conniving with the English Barons against King John, hoped to grasp the "key to the gateway of England" and subjugate us to French rule. Hubert de Burgh's brother, captured by the French at Norwich, was threatened with hanging unless the castle was surrendered. Hubert would not yield.

Prince Louis Phillipe, based at Dover Priory, was so moved by Hubert's defiance, that he refrained from hanging his brother. Instead, with siege engines and undermining tunnels, he breached the gateway structure. A desperate hand to hand battle followed. Hubert's men stood their ground. Prince Louis retreated to Lincoln. His luck ran out there too but the French did not give up the idea of conquest. Hubert was aware of this. With William Marshal, also a great loyal soldier he worked out a counter invasion plan.

The French were assembling a huge fleet, able to carry thousands of men, horses and siege engines. They had learned their shortcomings and although King John was dead, counted on Barons formerly in alliance with them. Henry III, in his minority, had William Marshal and Hubert de Burgh as regents. The fate of England was in their hands. What followed was extraordinary. That is why we should thankfully remember these great men. They shaped the nation's destiny.

Limekiln Street in 1217, was beside "Paradise", Dover's tidal harbour, when Hubert assembled his small fleet of "Cogs" – half the size of the French fleet under the command of Eustace the Monk, a much feared pirate, who was about to sail from Boulogne on the first fair wind. That wind was also on Hubert's mind. Providently he ordered hundreds of clay pots, suitable to be used as "sling shots", to be filled with quicklime readily available from limekilns nearby. Each Cog had "castles", rigged fore and aft, for crossbow teams.

William Marshal, with mounted knights and many foot soldiers were waiting to the North of Dover Castle, so as to deter the French from landing, keeping them on the move until the planned moment arrived.

On the morning of August 24th, 1217, on an ebb tide Hubert's Cogs set sail from Dover steering for Boulogne. To do this, the Cog's sails were reefed and tied so as to allow them to sail across the wind, while the tidal flow did the rest. Within two hours, both opposing fleets were in sight of each other, but did not attempt to engage. Having a fair wind, Eustace the Monk was soon off the White Cliffs of Dover. Hubert's fleet, out of sight un-reefed its sails as the tide began to rise and flow up the Strait of Dover. With wind and tide, the English Cogs made rapid progress towards Sandwich. The French were also heading that way.

Hubert de Burgh – a stained glass portrait at the entrance of the Maison Dieu, which he founded in 1203, to house pilgrims, the sick and others in need. St. Richard of Chichester died there in 1253. Hubert de Burgh, as Lord Warden of the Cinque Ports and Constable of Dover Castle, endowed this title with so much glory and honour, that since his day only one great person may hold it as a gift of the Sovereign. The Duke of Wellington, Sir Winston Churchill and Her Majesty, Queen Elizabeth, the Queen Mother, are among the recipients. The present Lord Warden is Admiral the Lord Boyce, a former head of NATO. Photo by Phil Wyborn-Brown.

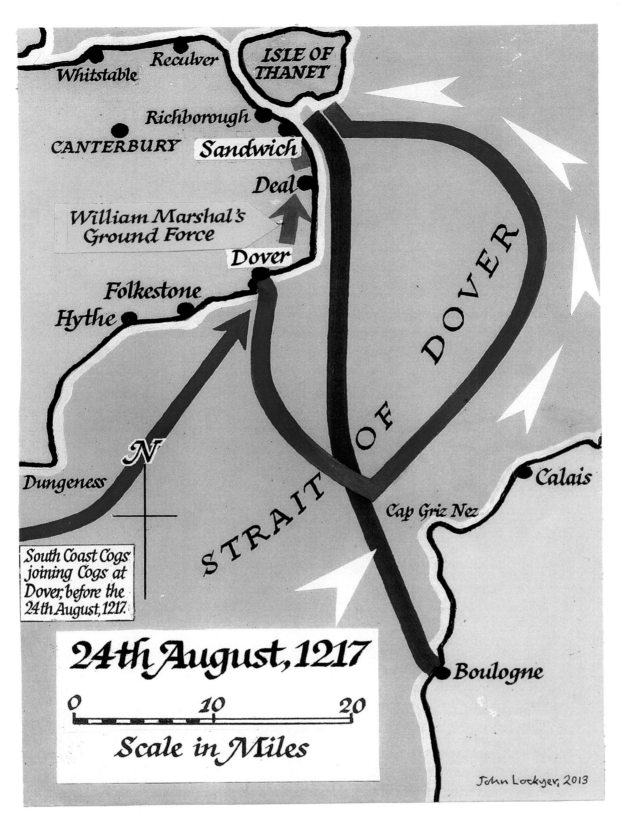

Reculver
Whitstable
ISLE OF THANET
Richborough
CANTERBURY
Sandwich
Deal
William Marshal's Ground Force
Dover
Folkestone
Hythe
STRAIT OF DOVER
Calais
Dungeness
Cap Griz Nez
South Coast Cogs joining Cogs at Dover, before the 24th August, 1217.

N

24th August, 1217

Boulogne

0   10   20

Scale in Miles

John Lockyer, 2013

Based on information from the "Met Office" and varying but helpful medieval records of "The Battle of Sandwich" I have drafted this highly probable plotting of movements by ships and men that rivals the victory of Trafalgar.

This powerful medieval image of William Marshal, sums up the situation before the Battle of Sandwich better than any words.

Eustace the Monk was soon aware that he had to avoid William Marshal's land force and get to Sandwich before they did. The arrival of Hubert de Burgh's unexpected fleet, added to the confusion. Eustace had everything against him as William Marshal's knights closed in and Hubert's Cogs began to form a parallel "line-ahead" attack formation, to deliver a broadside of quicklime as hundreds of slingshots created a blinding cloud that heralded a devastating storm of crossbow bolts. Eustace's men were helpless and he died, not in battle, but in captivity. Eustace was found hiding below the deck of his ship. Taken on deck, he was immediately beheaded. Later, the head was triumphantly paraded round Sandwich.

Hubert de Burgh's Cogs approaching Cap Gris Nez before changing course for Sandwich. An imagined masthead view portrayed by the author. Cogs were versatile and handy.

The Battle of Sandwich, like the Battle of Trafalgar, can be justly seen as historically important. It also gave the honour and glory to the title "Lord Warden of the Cinque Ports" – a singular honour that Hubert de Burgh gave substance to. While ferocious and seeming ruthless, he was also generously humane and devout. The Maison Dieu Hospital, Dover and Blackfriar's Monastery, London, were founded by him. I gladly admit, that Hubert stands as a "role model" for me. He is the true spirit of Dover. Those who determined the fate of Britian in the 1940's would have had Hubert de Burgh in mind.

So much of the Dover I knew – and most of the people I knew, are no more. This is not a lament but a challenge. History may relate a vanished past but the wondrous past of Dover is the future of prosperity of the town and its people. Let's use it!

While looking forward with confidence about the future of Dover, I enjoy thinking about the 1930's and writing about all of the things that made Dover special and exciting. I never tire of looking at these evocative images opposite.

These photographs taken by Rex Puttee, an Army Officer in Dover Garrison, were taken in 1939 before the outbreak of war. I can confirm this, as the ship berthed at the West end of Wellington Dock was well known to Snargate Street boys. It was registered in Trinidad as "Pacifico". Thanks to Rex Puttee we have a clear record of much swept away after 1939. Dover Prison and the special roadway cut into the East Cliff, had a major function in building the harbour. Old people I met as a boy told me how convicts in chains were marched down the cliff road every morning to make concrete blocks. These formed the inner core of the granite clad harbour walls.

The Train Ferry Berth, the old Harbour rail station and clock tower, together with the Viaduct, witness to the importance of the Admiralty Pier in the years between the wars. Up to five passenger ships could berth alongside the pier at one time. The Marine Station, with its magnificent entrance facade, ranks high as an architectural gem of the 20th Century. The nearby Victorian "Lord Warden Hotel", evokes the "Belle Epoch" when Anglo-French relations began to flourish and paddle steamers went to and fro. Admiralty Pier is popular for those who enjoy fishing or just watching the waves. Remember, some of those waves can be dangerous while awe inspiring, so take care.

"Archcliffe Gate" was built with many other urgent improvements to Dover's defences on the "Western Heights", in the 1850's - a bonanza for "navvies" and bricklayers, which became known as "Palmerston's Folly", Road widening a hundred years later put an end to this splendid gateway. What a shame. Photo, Dover Museum.

Beyond the foreshore

PART 9

Since I began writing this book, family and friends suggested that I should include an account of the first nine months of the Second World War. I am persuaded to do this. The evacuation of Dunkirk combined with the consequent evacuation of Dover's schoolchildren on Sunday, June 1st, 1940, was an important turning point for me.

From the time of the 1938 Munich crisis, Dover was preparing for war. Fishing trawlers arrived, to be converted as minesweepers. Trainloads of guns and other warlike equipment could be seen at docksides in Dover, enabling this to happen. The 350ft pylons at Swingate–high ground to the East of the Castle, then a mystery, were also foreboding. Gas masks were already distributed. Air raid precautions were on cigarette cards. Archie Wellden was already an Air Raid Warden, long before Sunday, September 3rd, 1939. He proudly wore his Warden's badge at school.

That fateful day was fine and sunny. My parents told me that an important radio announcement would be made while I was at St. Mary's Church. They trusted that when the time came, I would obey instructions. It was so unfamiliar and unreal – yet it was otherwise a normal Dover Sunday – shop windows covered with white blinds, marked "Dean of Putney" and Church bells happily ringing as I reached my destination. Seated opposite me in the Choir Stalls (the "cantori" side) was J.J. Smith, a school friend with whom I am still in contact, while I was on the "decani" side not far from the organ console. Then the service began.

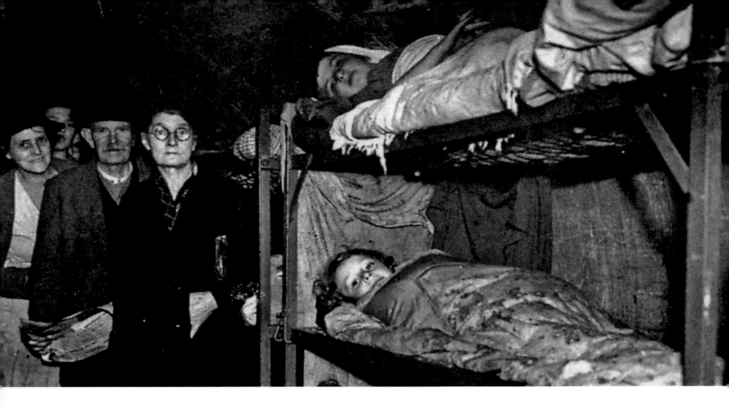

Caves – originally used as "bonded warehouses", were well used by the time of Dunkirk. They gave much to the morale of people throughout the period of Dover's "Front Line" status, lasting nearly four years. Photo, Dover Museum.

Within minutes, a sidesman approached the vicar's stall, handing him a slip of paper. The Reverend Ritchie gave a nod to Leonard Baggerly, the organist – who immediately stopped playing. The dreaded news of war was delivered to the congregation as Air Raid Sirens began howling. So this was it! "Stay in this church – you'll be safer here", urged the vicar.

"Baggy" the choirmaster and organist, glanced along the stalls to make sure that his "tadpoles" had not fled for cover as the service continued. J.J. Smith's father prudently brought his son's gas mask to the North door – just in case. However, the enemy did not come. The "all clear" siren came and everyone made their way home safely.

My parents were busily preparing for all kinds of war emergencies. "Barwicks Cave" would be our air raid shelter. All our family necessities were packed ready for a hasty exit. Everyone living in Snargate Street ventured to discuss the topic of shelters, making grim necessity a part of social life. This would eventually help to reduce the casualty rate in Dover, as later records suggest.

*The Radar Pylons at Swingate – officially known as "Swingate Chain
Home Station", photographed in 1939 were the successors of the original
experimental wooden pylons, erected in 1938 a short distance to the
right of this picture. Both sets of pylons were used during the war.
Radar (Radio Location) enabled swift deployment of fighter aircraft – a
vital factor in the outcome of the Battle of Britain. The four swingate
pylons – each nearly 350 feet high, were impressive sentinels – two
still survive, having served beyond the war in military communication
and television transmission. A chain of 47 similar sites existed round
Britain during the Second World War. Photo, Dover Museum.*

The first day of war, with beautiful weather, somehow kindled a sense of hope and defiance. With my parents and two sisters, I proudly wore my first pair of long trousers, as with other Dovorians we strolled along our beloved seafront, gasmasks in clean cardboard cases, slung over our shoulders on white string. Hoping to spot an enemy aircraft or submarine, I took with me a five shilling telescope bought from Brewingtons, the Bench Street toyshop.

Surprisingly, many people were bathing or swimming. So quiet did it seem in Dover, in the early days of the war, that it became a reception area for evacuees from London. Dover Borough Council thought it advisable to warn London children of natural local hazards – cliffs and strong sea currents. The Londoners, with ample supplies of chalk, made this reply to molly-coddling authority. "Dover Sharks, sitting on the grass, shooting peas at a nanny goat's arse". Most Londoners returned home. The "phoney war" lasted for months.

The B.E.F. – British Expeditionary Force, intent on "hanging out its washing on the Siegfried line", was seen off by Dover boys before winter set in. The real war in 1939 was at sea. German mines or torpedoes were taking their toll in the Channel. We soon had hard evidence of that when we went beachcombing one early Saturday morning with the tide coming in. To our delight and surprise, large rectangular objects were rapidly coming towards us. Using my telescope I could see that these were teachests.

Somehow we managed to get strong paper bags and cardboard boxes ready to hold this unexpected treasure – tea being rationed – plus a small hatchet and a jemmy to open the chests. We managed to open two teachests and save several unspoilt pounds of tea, before the Customs Men spotted us. Seawater had caused a watertight outer barrier of tealeaves to protect about two thirds of the chest contents. But what did the Customs Men do? They didn't bother us at all!

With a motor launch at their disposal, they were able to retrieve dozens of teachests. Hacking them open, they dumped everything into the sea. The "Dover Tea Party" was a futile gesture, while our mothers enjoyed the tea that had probably cost men's lives. Sinkings were frequent. The sunken Union Castle Line, *Dunbar Castle's* lifeboats were linked together and towed into the Western end of the harbour. I watched this happening. Later, the lifeboats were taken to Wellington Dock.

Another shocking reminder of the war at sea was the Varne Lightship, shattered by cannon shells from attacking enemy aircraft. It was moored on the North side of Wellington Dock. Dover people could see that it was not a "phoney war" by the time Christmas 1939 came.

"The Nook" had customers who had seen action at sea – officers and men serving on minesweepers or destroyers, also soldiers, armed with rifles came. *HMS Skipjack*, a trawler converted to minesweeping, brought us "regular customers" when tied up in the Tidal Harbour – a dangerous place for members of crew returning in the blackout as the tide dropped. Sadly, alcohol could lead to a fall, serious injury or death.

Soldiers and sailors thronged Snargate Street when off duty. The Royal Hippodrome next to where we lived above my father's restaurant, was then the centrepiece of the street. Its management, no doubt wishing to appeal to the tastes of lusty sailors and soldiers, had almost abandoned the traditional music-hall programmes for which the theatre had been well known, in favour of posing nudes. These ladies, usually claimed to be "from the *Folies Bergère*", rejoicing in names such as Drina or Peaches Weston. By an oversight no doubt, on the part of my parents, I saw Drina not on the Hippodrome stage so much as off it. That evening, as the stage curtains were drawn back to the tune "Lovely Lady", revealing the still nude pose of Drina, something dreadful took place. Not only did Drina move, contrary to the rules of the Lord Chamberlain, but so did the whole of the scenery in which the nude lady was seated. The disaster, not due to enemy action, caused the audience to gasp.

Sailors in the front row of the stalls rose to give assistance as Drina vanished in a welter of broken woodwork and drapery. As the orchestra died, the safety curtain swiftly fell into place and the auditorium became a buzz of voices. Presently the theatre manager, Mr Armstrong, in evening dress, appeared over the footlights to assure everyone that all was well, including Drina. With a wave of a hand he then beckoned to Drina, now decently clad in a pink dressing gown, to howls and whistles from servicemen. The disrupted evening at the Hippodrome was concluded with rousing choruses of "Roll out the barrel" and "There'll always be an England". Others have quoted from my 1990 account.

1940, the fateful New Year, began with a big freeze. The clatter of chained wheels on ice covered roads, was more familiar than sounds of explosions at sea. Because many look-out troops manned cliff-tops, boys would beg their mothers for hot drinks in thermos flasks, so as to support the look-outs. I went with Fearnley Parsons and Dennis Willet to a look-out post on Shakespeare Cliff. The men there were glad to see us. Later we visited their base – a tented camp a short distance from the "King Lear" public house. It was a cold war.

When my father began work at the Garrison Officer's Mess in 1940, he closed The Nook. We went to live at 2 Last Lane, a large Georgian house owned by Mr Greenstreet, one of the choirmen at St. Mary's Church. We rented a comfortable flat there. School was almost next door. As winter passed, things began to happen across the Channel and air raid warnings became more frequent. I made many visits to anti-aircraft gun sites.

As the German break-through came, it was clear that invasion threatened. My father kept up with the latest news. Every evening, I went with him to Market Square nearby, where he bought an Evening Standard. Distant rumbling – not thunder, but sounds of battle, could be heard. "They say that the Germans have taken Arras", said my father – "but they are closer than that" he added. I put my hand against a plate glass window. It was shaking. Our men across the Channel were in trouble. Dunkirk was their only way out. It was Britain's darkest hour.

Dunkirk, Vice-Admiral Sir Bertram Ramsay, Flag Officer, Dover, checks the availability of ships in his rescue fleet – especially destroyers. The last week in May, 1940, was agonising. It is an ironical fact that Vera Lynn had just recorded one of her best–loved songs "It's a lovely day tomorrow". Photo, Dover Museum.

One evening I shall never forget, is after a visit to an anti-aircraft gunsite on the East Cliff seafront. The soldiers were busy setting fuses, so that the shells would burst at fixed altitudes. I was walking home, past the Burlington and Granville Gardens. As I turned right at the Shalimar Hotel, a "Bofors" Light anti-aircraft gun opened fire. The gun was in the hotel front garden. The sound was deafening

Arriving home, my mother gave me some "Aspro" tablets. "The Germans are coming", she said while opening the large sash windows of the living room. Sure enough, anti-aircraft shells were bursting over the East Cliff Lookout Point – then we heard the bangs. Father took charge. Mother, my two sisters and I, were ordered to take cover below the stairway, close to the chimney structure. "This is less likely to collapse", father said. We obeyed.

My boyish curiosity took over from apprehension or fear. I wanted to see what was happening. In a few moments, I was in the living room again (on some lame excuse). The sky was darkened between vivid flashes of bursting anti-aircraft shells. Naval searchlight beams began to entrap the intruders – minelaying Dover Harbour. One beam was becoming horizontal, together with a stream of tracer bullets. Then with a roar of aero-engines, a Heinkel III bomber came into momentary view, less than 300 feet away at rooftop level! It was trying to escape destruction. The rivets on its fuselage were points of reflected lights as it headed inland, escorted by tracer bullets and "pom-pom" shells. Then came the lull. With eiderdowns wrapped over our heads, we went quickly to Barwicks Cave. Halfway to our shelter in Snargate Street, firing began again. Shrapnel was clattering on rooftops. I felt very scared, as this was lethal, but somehow this gave way to anger. I wanted a gun to blaze away at my tormentors. A young mother near us, was dragging a screaming toddler along while dropping everything else she had. A kindly air raid warden came to her aid. That night, stray tracer bullets set fire to a school-friends dog kennel. The dog was safe in a shelter.

Operation Dynamo was reaching its climax. Every spare moment was spent with other boys, watching the ships coming into every available landing place with thousands of soldiers, many of whom were wounded. From a viewpoint near the Drop Redoubt, you could see how awful it was. With such a desperate need of ambulances, those at the disposal of the Army and Navy were insufficient. One remarkable solution was found, as Dover Corporation had a permanent contract with the East Kent Road Car Company. Single deck buses, in every way saved the day, and many lives. Another miracle of Dunkirk? Yes, let me explain.

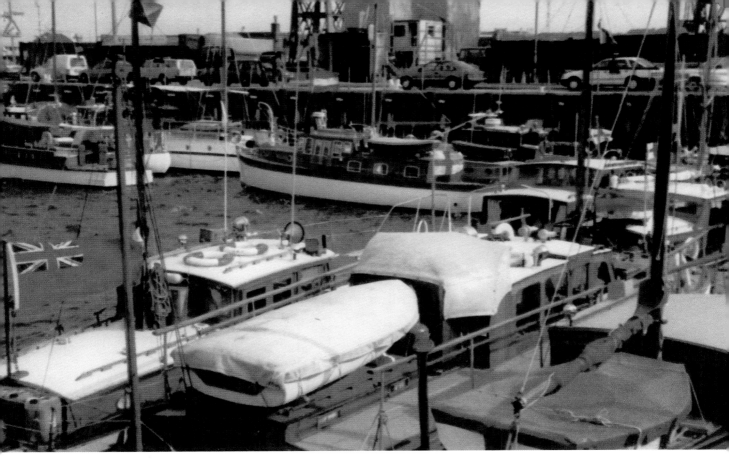

The "little ships" of Dunkirk, gathered in June, 1990, in Wellington Dock, Dover, for the 50th anniversary of the evacuation. Although quite a number of these "little ships" made repeated crossings, most were used to ferry troops to larger vessels that could not get close to the shoreline. Many little ship men died. Photo, the author

With a spacious rear emergency exit and two rows of seats, a single deck bus could take at least six stretchers, while the luggage racks could enable blood transfusion equipment or drips to be used. I saw such a converted bus at close quarters. Seen at a distance, the line of "East Kent" bus ambulances on the Prince of Wales Pier, with their red coachwork, made an unforgettable scene with the sea, jade green and smooth, on which grey minesweepers laden with khaki uniformed men, moved in turn to a flight of steps on the pier's stone extension. Awaiting the stretcher-bound wounded, who were disembarked first, was the line of red East Kent bus ambulances. They stretched shorewards on the girder section of the pier. I remember that a St Mary's schoolboy drew a picture of this. Surprisingly, I may be the only person who bothered to report this aspect of the evacuation of Dunkirk. There is a good reason for this.

Admiralty Pier was the main landing place at the time. Dramatic events there overshadowed what was elsewhere. My father, as a Great War veteran, served as a volunteer, in a horrific circumstance, while working on Admiralty Pier. A small cargo ship arrived in Dover in a sinking condition. Its forward hold had received a direct hit by a German bomb. The hold was full of soldiers, most of whom died. With other volunteers, my father sorted out the survivors of this carnage and took them ashore on stretchers. He appears briefly in a newsreel sequence, wearing his "Battersby" trilby hat.

Two days later, while digging a clifftop machine gun trench, the Battersby hat was torn apart by a German bullet. My father, then in his sixties, dropped his trilby while taking cover. German machine gunning was a hazard for many. I will always remember how upset my father was about his hat, when he came home that day.

Invasion seemed inevitable. Land mines and barbed wire soon made beaches out of bounds. My last swim near the Clock Tower, was two hours before the mines were planted and barbed wire garlanded the beach. Fortunately I was out of the sea and dressed before a duet of machine gun fire and an aero engine made me dash for cover in a public toilet. Most of my companions took cover undressed. No one was harmed.

Before Dunkirk fell, normal schooling was impossible. Air raid shelters are not classrooms. On the last Friday in May, 1940, we were told to prepare for evacuation to South Wales. Our parents had been urged to consent, although they could refuse. Next day, Saturday, I received a letter from "Aspro Limited". Unknown to me, my mother had sent a drawing of mine, showing anti-aircraft gunners being dosed with "Aspro" Tablets. With the letter, came a book, "The Rifle Rangers" by Captain Mayne Reid. This was the only book that I was able to take with me as an evacuee.

The seventieth anniversary service of thanksgiving of Dover schoolchildren evacuated to South Wales. Left – the author interviewed before the service by the BBC at St. Mary the Virgin Church. Right – in the Stone Hall of the Maison Dieu, for cream teas, more BBC interviews and songs, accompanied by piano.

Sunday, June 1st – no church that day! As a school we marched to Dover Priory Station, carrying luggage with large labels round our necks and our gasmasks. Mothers were on the pavement, waving farewell or weeping. I last saw my mother, wearing a lilac and white knitted cardigan. At Dover Priory Station, we faced the unknown – the end of childhood – an adventure and a challenge. Taking the North Kent Line, our train entered the tunnel. Clouds of steam underlined our uncertainty. I buried all my thoughts in my new book. Other boys nicknamed me "Aspro" on that long journey. I didn't mind that.

Reunited evacuees – eleven days after arriving in Blaenavon, South Wales. The author, 12, with his sisters – L. Rosetta, 5 and R. Primrose, 9. This was the first time the author met his sisters again, after evacuation. Thanks to Marie Jenkins, a lovely 16 year old Welsh girl.

From the invitation to the thanksgiving on June 6th 2010, "Seventy years on". From a "Brownie" snapshot by Marie Jenkins, June 12th, 1940.

Fourteen hours on a train, repeatedly shunted into sidings, to give urgent troop trains priority in the prospect of enemy invasion, was not a pleasant experience. Nor was it pleasant for the people of the South Wales valleys, suddenly called upon to take us children into their homes. Much has been said of my love for Dover. The same is true regarding South Wales. Through Mr Wellden, the St Mary's School for Boys headmaster, I was able to benefit from the Welsh education system, which opened many doors of opportunity.

By the time I was sixteen, I was a freelancer making sets of heraldic designs for an art dealer. My studies for a National Design Diploma included work for exhibitions connected with planned post-war recovery. When the ambitious Patrick Abercrombie plans for the rebuilding of London, were published in 1943, they became an important part of my studies at Newport Technical College. The knowledge and practical ability that I gained, enabled me to lead successful opposition at planning enquiries, against speculative land revaluation.

Thanks to Wales, I had a career which involved the theatre, film – also television and advertising. I worked for the late Sir David Frost for over 40 years. Mrs Whitehouse "head hunted" me as an advisor Through Robert de Wynter, Andrew Lloyd Webber's publicist, I had to write as the "Phantom", invitations to the New York Premiere of the famous musical, again – all thanks to Wales. At the time (1988), I was calligrapher to St. Paul's Cathedral Dean and Chapter.

One great sadness, while studying in South Wales, was the death of my younger sister, Rosetta, killed by an Army lorry in 1944. It was in the run up to "D Day". Rosetta at 9 years, had a lovely singing voice. Weeks before this, she sang at a concert for hundreds of war workers – "The White Cliffs of Dover". I have told Dame Vera Lynn about this. She loves Dover and is keenly interested in its future prospects.

I have done some crazy things in my boyhood. The stretch of Dover coastline, "Samphire Hoe", was once a jumble of large chalk boulders. By 1939, as an athletic 11 year old I developed a silly and dangerous lone pastime – boulder running. You leapt from boulder to boulder (not covered by seaweed) – making split-second decisions as to which boulders you could take at a run. Being alone, an accident could be disastrous for me but I had confidence – and still have it! I welcome chances and challenges. The rest of my story depends on you. Do you care about Dover? Thank you – I am not alone. Others are no less enthusiastic and unlike me, an exile, live in or close to Dover. The eighth centenary commemorations, 2015, 2016 and 2017, should be a challenging opportunity for like-minded people.

Thanks are due to Terry Sutton, M.B.E., for prompting "Beyond the foreshore" during a telephone conversation in 2012 and for sustaining his interest and support in my preparations for publication. I had warm encouragement from my old school friend and fellow boy chorister, J.J. Smith. Also, special thanks to St. Mary the Virgin Church P.C.C. Among others who have provided me with valuable assistance, Dame Vera Lynn, and Derek Leach, O.B.E. The Hollingsbee Collection, The Imperial War Museum, and National Maritime Museum, Phil Wyborn-Brown, Dover Museum and Library, Kent Archives, The Dover Society and Dover Harbour Board, deserve my thanks. Since my draft was in longhand, also because I do not have computer skills, I am glad to give special thanks to a family friend and carer – June Dufaur. She made things happen – which I hope this little book will do.

Above all, the patience of my dear wife, Kathleen, enabled me to have time to get things done. While this book has taken eighteen months to prepare, Kathleen has had to put up with me and my very busy life for over fifty-nine years. This being so, I dedicate this labour of love to her.

Although my working life required me to live in London, I spent time in Dover whenever possible. The bugler's platform is at the top right of this 1950 photograph, taken by the author.

POSTSCRIPT

On the veranda of the "White Cliffs" hotel. June, 1988. Photo, the author.

Gareth Malone, O.B.E., created choirs which competed with each other in 2013. They were each made up from employees of major organisations or businesses. P and O Ferries Dover, won the contest, which was covered by BBC television. This achievement has revived a notion of mine, that ferry companies could be the nucleus of Anglo-European cultural relations. Until the 6th March, 1987, when the *"Herald of Free Enterprise"* capsized after leaving the Belgian port of Zebrugge, I regarded Townsend Thoresen as an "ace" for such an idea. Thank you P and O Ferries for cementing a foundation stone with Gareth Malone to "make Dover over" as the "City of European Accord", in music.

Dover a City? Yes, Dover has a bishop. Should he choose to have his Throne – his "Cathedra", in the Chancel of Saint Mary the Virgin Church, Cannon Street, Dover could in time qualify as a City! Since size is a misleading qualification for City status, the administrative area of "Dover and District Council" begs a positive answer. Let's have it before the Eight Hundredth Anniversary of the Siege of Dover Castle. I have been encouraged by ideas that have been seriously considered by others concerning Dover's future. They are both imaginative and commercially viable and come from members of The Dover Society – of which I am very glad to be a member.

Aspirations of life ultimately need hard cash. I soon grasped this essential principle when I wanted to go fishing and needed equipment to do this. Pocket money – a penny a day, also the regular chorister payment which started at one pound a year, was insufficient. With Fearnley Parsons, I found the answer. We built a handcart, capable of holding a good load of discarded glass bottles and jars. These were washed clean, with labels all removed – ready for sale to a scrap merchant in Peter Street. This was a regular Saturday job, which gained at least six shillings once a month. We were into "recycling". It paid.

These combined financial resources made all the difference and sustained a happy boyhood. While monetary values have changed in my lifetime, the recycling principle remains. Recycling Dover should be a priority today. That's very much in accord with intentions to improve port facilities, as Dover Harbour Board have made known, provided that the port and town are an inseparable whole. Prospective investors, please grasp a wonderful once in a lifetime opportunity awaiting in Dover that could surprise the World and delight you. Go for it then!

John Lockyer 2014

INDEX

Eastern Arm, 5. East Kent Bus Ambulances, 78, 79. Elizabeth I, queen, 14. English Heritage, 30, 62. Eton Collars, 45. Eustace the Monk, 63. Evacuation of children, 80–83. Extension, (Admiralty Pier), 50.

Fan Bay, 4, 5. Faring Boats, 34, 35, 36. Ferry Berth problems, 43. Fire alarm emergency, 59. Firing Range, 31. Fowler Train Ferry proposal, 47. Frost, Sir David, 83.

Gateway to England. 3. George V, king, 53. German timber imports, 53. "Gestapo" (school yard game), 53. Gigg and Tournay, outfitters, 3, 56. Glatton, H.M.S., 6, 7, 8. Golden Arrow Service, 50, 51. Graf Zeppelin airship, 53. Grand Shaft, 37, 38, 39. Granville Dock, 15, 16, 17. Granville Gardens, 53. Grand Hotel, 53. Great Pier of Henry VIII, 13, 16, 48. Guns, 61.

Harmonium, 45. "Haughty Belle", spritsail barge, 16, 17. Hawkesfields, coal wharf, 16. Hazards entering port, 50. "Herald of Free Enterprise", 86. Holy Week, 27. Homelife, 42. Hudson's Passage, 30. Human Rights, 9.

Immigrants (illegal), 62. Invasion, French attempt, 62, 63.

John, king of England, 62. Juvenile delinquency, 18.

Keep, admission to, 28. Keyes, Sir Roger, Vice Admiral, 7.

"Lady Brassey" and "Lady Duncannon", tugs, 6, 9. "Lady Saville", passenger tender, 13. Launching – landing, rowing boats, 36. Leach, Derek, O.B.E., 30. Lear, king, (Shakespeare), 40. Lee-Enfield rifles, 31. Lighters (work boats), 16. Limekiln Street, 49, 63. Lincoln, battle of, 62. Lockyer, Kathleen, Mrs, 32, 33, 34, 86. Lockyer, Primrose, sister, 11, 37, 54, 55, 56, 57, 58, 82. Lockyer, Rosetta, sister, 53, 58, 60. London Evacuees in Dover, 74. Lookout posts on clifftops, 76. Louis Phillipe, prince, 62. "Love on the dole", drama, 50. Lord Warden (Cinque Ports), 13, 64. Lord Warden Hotel, 41. Loyalty, 23. Lynn, Dame Vera, 77, 83.

BIBLIOGRAPHY

Compiled with the assistance of Dover Museum and The Dover Society, to compliment "Beyond the Foreshore". Books marked with an asterisk, can be purchased from Dover Museum Shop. Otherwise, the Public Library Service, in conjunction with The British Library should be able to help you.

* TOWNWALL STREET DOVER EXCAVATIONS, 1996 (Hardback £25) ISBN 1-870545-052. The Bronze Age Boat, preserved in Dover Museum, is an eloquent witness of trade with mainland Europe more than 3500 years ago.

   THE HISTORY OF DOVER HARBOUR by Alec Hansenson, 1980. (Hardback), price may vary around £45–£50. This is a well written and well-illustrated book of nearly 500 pages. To sum-up, it is an inspiring account of human endeavour. Published by Aurum Special Editions, 11 Garrick Street, London, WC2. ISBN 0-906053-17X.

* THE ROMAN HOUSE WITH BACCHIC MURALS AT DOVER. (Hardback) £22.40. ISBN 0-947831-06-1. This remarkable house is believed to be a hotel for cross channel travellers – mostly imperial officials. Very stimulating to the imagination.

* THE DISCOVERY AND EXCAVATION OF ANGLO SAXON DOVER, (Hardback) ISBN 0-947831-231, £25.20. This will make you want to know more!

* KINGDOM KEY DOVER IN WORDS AND PICTURES ISBN 0-9517577-1-7, £45. So you can understand why people fall in love with Dover. I have!

* THE STREETS OF DOVER by Derek Leach – a man who did fall in love with the place. Derek, an OBE, is Chairman of The Dover Society as well as an accomplished historian. This book is

essential if you have caught the "Dover bug". For your cure, join The Dover Society. Contact the Membership Secretary now – 01304 211308 (Mrs Sheila Cope).
This book – ISBN 978-0-9536166-8-8, is £12.99.

* Mr DOVER REPORTING by Terry Sutton, M.B.E. ISBN 978-0-9536166-7-1, £10. The instigator of my book, Terry Sutton, has a lifetime record of his profession as an outstanding journalist. This book fills in details about Dover's history in my adult lifetime when I was elsewhere. As an exile Dovorian, I have enjoyed reading Terry's reporting. I am glad to add, that there's more to come from him!

* THE WHITE CLIFFS OF DOVER by Peter and Julie Burville. ISBN 09539478-1-5. Are there bluebirds over the white cliffs? With modern media "apps" there will be. Meanwhile, "Images of Cliff and Shore" by the Burvilles, priced £8.75, will conjure Dame Vera Lynn's unforgettable voice for you – and more!

Dover will always remember with pride, the man, HUBERT de BURGH. Clarence Ellis, a truly dedicated historian and biographer, sub-titled his stirring and well annotated book, published by Phoenix House in 1952 – before ISBN numbering:- "A Study in Constancy". That supreme human quality is evident in every part of Hubert de Burgh's life. Your local Public Library, in conjunction with The British Library, can help you to obtain this great book. Also enquire through The Union Publishing Group, Flat 22, 27 Hardwicks Way, London SW18 4AL.

WILLIAM MARSHAL – Knight Errant Baron & Regent of England. By Sidney Painter. Barnes & Nobel Books, New York, U.S.A. ISBN 1-55619-734-1. This brilliant insight into medieval society gives you a greater appreciation of how our modern institutions began. William Marshal and Hubert de Burgh were instrumental in this process as loyal servants to the young Plantagenet King, Henry III.

*   DOVER IN THE SECOND WORLD WAR
By Terry Sutton and Derek Leach. Published by Philimore &
Co. Ltd. Andover Hants, gives a vivid account of Britain's front
line town and its people. The co–authorship – by two notable
Dovorians, ensures accurate details as they are both leading
members of The Dover Society. ISBN 978.1.86077.61.9.

*   DOVER 1945 – 2000 – Our Town Dover
By Terry Sutton and Derek Leach. Published by Riverdale Ltd.
River, Dover, Kent CT17 0QX. An appropriate companion and
sequel to their wartime account. Terry and Derek are witnesses
to Dover's changes. ISBN 09536166.4.9.

DOVER'S FORGOTTEN FORTRESS
The Western Heights
By Janice Welby
Published by Kent County Library
The "hidden city" for adventurous boys – but out of bounds. This
book is well written and illustrated. It argues how important it
is that the Western Heights should be preserved for posterity.
ISBN 0.90.515543.2

The Guide Book to Dover Castle, English Heritage, is an excellent
reference to the "key" to the "Gateway of England" obtainable at the
Castle shop.